The Fair Prenup

Protecting Your Legacy Without Leaving Your Partner Behind

Dera G. Madueke

This book is provided for informational and educational purposes only. Nothing contained herein should be construed as legal advice specific to your situation. Laws vary by jurisdiction, and the application of legal principles can differ depending on individual facts and circumstances. The author and publisher make no representations or warranties regarding the accuracy, completeness, or applicability of the material to your particular case.

If you require legal advice tailored to your needs, please consult a licensed attorney in your city or jurisdiction. The author and publisher expressly disclaim any liability for actions taken or not taken based on the contents of this publication.

Contents

Introduction

No one walks into a relationship dreaming about contracts. Most people don't sit across from someone they love and imagine having to negotiate what happens if it all falls apart. But that is exactly why so many people find themselves in quiet confusion, deep resentment, or total emotional collapse years later. They never asked the questions that mattered because love was supposed to be enough.

But love does not cancel out reality. Love does not erase what came before. It does not rewrite the will. It does not change the title deed. And it certainly does not guarantee that both people will walk away protected, respected, and seen.

This book started with a woman who sat in my office and told me she was tired. Not of her husband, not of love, not even of the challenges that come with marriage, but of the quiet imbalance that had begun to eat away at her. She had left her job, moved into his home, helped raise his children, and supported his business. She showed up every day for a life he had built before she arrived, and she gave herself to it without hesitation. But somewhere along the way, she started to wonder whether she had ever truly belonged in it.

She did not want to take anything from him. She was not trying to override his children's inheritance or claim what was not hers. She simply wanted to know that she mattered in a way that could not be erased. She wanted her sacrifices to mean something. She wanted to feel like more than a placeholder. And most of all, she wanted to know that if he died before her, she would not be left with nothing after giving so much.

That moment stayed with me. It forced me to rethink everything I had seen and heard around the topic of prenups. It reminded me that fairness is not only about assets or balance sheets. Fairness is about recognition. It is about how we protect one another while still protecting ourselves. It is about writing agreements that reflect love, not suspicion. It is about knowing the difference between protecting your past and building your future.

This book is not a legal manual, though the legal clarity is here. It is not a relationship advice book, though it will absolutely help save some. It is a guide for those who want to enter into marriage with their eyes open, their values intact, and their dignity unshaken.

If you are someone who has sacrificed without acknowledgment, this book is for you. If you are someone who has assets and wants to protect them without becoming controlling, this book is for you too. And if you are somewhere in between, still figuring out how to love fully without losing yourself, this book will help you find language, structure, and strength.

This is not about fighting for power, but claiming your place with calm, intelligent conviction. It is about knowing what you bring to the table, even if it is not written in dollar signs. And it is about making sure that love is not the reason you are left with nothing when you gave everything. This is *The Fair Prenup*.

ONE

When Love Meets Legacy

1. The house is beautiful, but it doesn't feel like home

A house can be filled with sunlight, expensive rugs, and curated art. You can move through its rooms every day, open its drawers, cook in its kitchen, and still feel like you do not live there. Not really. You sleep there. You clean it. You may even care for the people in it. But something is missing that no furniture can give you.

It is the feeling that you are allowed to exist fully in a space that belongs to you just as much as it belongs to the person beside you.

This is what many women feel but rarely explain well. The structure may be flawless. The location might be perfect. The mortgage may be paid off. But emotionally, it feels rented. You are not decorating, you are tiptoeing. You are not building, you are managing what has already been built. And with every passing year, you wonder how long you can do this before you begin to disappear inside it.

A lot of men don't understand this. Especially the ones who see themselves as providers. They think giving you shelter is the same thing as giving you a home. They don't notice what it feels like to live among memories that do not include you. They do not feel what it means to improve someone else's legacy with your time and care, while knowing it will never have your name on it. It is not about taking something away, but about needing to see yourself in the life you are helping hold up.

Some women enter marriages where the house is already there. The history is already there. The future has already been written. And yet they show up with their hands, their presence, their effort, hoping to be folded in. Hoping to belong. But when the terms are never discussed, when nothing is promised or protected, the message becomes obvious over time. This life is his. You are only here for now.

This is where emotional erosion begins. Not with one big betrayal, but with repeated small messages that say, over and over again, you do not have a permanent claim to this place. And if you don't have a claim to where you live, it becomes harder to believe you have one in the relationship itself. Being generous with love is not the same thing as being careless with your future. If you have made a life inside someone else's structure, if you've contributed to something that wasn't originally yours, you deserve more than a verbal 'thank you'. You deserve legal and emotional security that matches your contribution. A home is more than walls. It is also the feeling that you can stay.

2. Loving someone with a life that started without you

You may fall in love with someone who had a life in motion long before you arrived. He already had a home. He had routines. Maybe even children, investments, or traditions you were never part of creating. And now you are expected to fit into that life without disturbing it too much. No one talks about how strange that can feel. You are not just joining a person. You are joining their story mid-chapter. The early pages were written without your voice. Sometimes that means navigating a family dynamic that feels closed to you. Other times, it means adapting to rules that were never discussed, because everyone else already knows them.

You might hear, "this is how we do things," or, "this is the way it's always been." But those sentences are not explanations. They are barriers. And over time, you begin to understand that you were invited into this life, but not necessarily included in shaping it.

This dynamic does not always come from malice. In many cases, the man you love has simply been functioning in survival or provider mode for so long that he no longer recognizes how much control he is holding. He believes he is sharing his world with you, but in truth, he may only be offering space within it, not ownership, not voice, not co-authorship. This is where many women start to feel tension they cannot name. You may begin to notice that decisions are being made without you. That family holidays are planned around his traditions. That conversations about assets, property, or the future happen in past tense, as if they are already settled. You are here, but you are not part of the structure. Even when there is kindness, even when there is affection, this quiet exclusion can feel like a form of erasure. You may start to question your instincts. You ask yourself whether you are asking for too much. You wonder whether your discomfort is legitimate or just insecurity. But deep down, you know what is happening. You are being asked to fold into a life that has no intention of bending for you.

Healthy relationships are built on shared growth. If one person brings their full history and the other is expected to shrink around it, that is not a partnership. That is proximity. You can love someone and still need space to grow beside them. You can respect their past without surrendering your right to shape the present. If you are entering a relationship where the structure is already built, then fairness means being allowed to help choose what gets renovated, what gets preserved, and what is built next.

The hard part isn't that the life existed before you. It's that sometimes, it continues to exist as if you haven't arrived.

A lady I met shared with me how, during Thanksgiving, she suggested a new side dish. Something simple. Something from her own childhood. But it wasn't really paid any attention. She told me she didn't even care about the food. What hurt was realizing how little space she had to bring her own story into the mix. She only wanted to be allowed to leave her fingerprint somewhere in the life she was now part of. That's the silent weight many women carry in these relationships. You are expected to love fully, but not shape anything. To support completely, but not influence direction. You are allowed to show up, but not change the furniture. Metaphorically and sometimes literally.

And it gets more complicated when finances are involved. If he already owns the house, already set up the trust, already has a plan for where everything goes, you start to feel like someone who arrived late to the meeting. You're present, but not part of the decision-making.

Some women accept it quietly. Some push back. Others float somewhere in between, not sure if they are being too demanding or too invisible. The truth is, neither extreme is healthy. A relationship that requires you to disappear in order to keep peace is not a relationship that sees you as equal. Loving someone with a history is not the issue. The issue is whether that history is allowed to grow, or if it is frozen in place with no room for your influence.

You can honor his past and still ask for your voice to matter. You can respect what he's built and still be part of building what comes next. Love does not require silence. It asks for presence. And presence, in its truest form, requires participation.

3. Why silence about money always turns into noise later

When couples avoid talking about money, it rarely creates peace. It only creates delay. The silence might feel like harmony in the beginning, but it almost always builds into confusion, and eventually, resentment.

Money is not just a number in a bank account. It is tied to safety, to power, to autonomy. When it is left unspoken, people start to make private assumptions. Those assumptions eventually shape behavior, and those behaviors, over time, start to feel like betrayal.

In many relationships, especially where one person has significantly more assets than the other, conversations about money feel uncomfortable. People don't want to sound greedy. They don't want to appear calculating. And so they stay quiet. They tell themselves that love should be bigger than contracts. That trust means not needing to ask what happens next. But deep down, they are often negotiating with themselves in private. Asking questions they are too afraid to bring up. Imagining scenarios they are too polite to voice. That silence becomes its own kind of tension.

And when something finally brings those hidden thoughts to the surface - an illness, a disagreement, a will, a child's reaction; things that could have been calmly discussed at the beginning now explode with emotion. Instead of talking about values, couples find themselves arguing about intentions. Instead of building together, they are defending their position. What could have been handled with transparency becomes a fight for clarity that now feels like a test of loyalty. Do not think that avoiding the topic of money will preserve love, it only delays conflict. Financial silence does not protect a relationship. It just buries the hard questions until they resurface in worse conditions.

Nobody benefits from living inside someone else's financial plan without knowing what that plan actually is. It may feel noble to trust, to say nothing, to go with the flow. But trust without information is not intimacy. It is blind dependence. And that is a fragile place to build a life from.

When a woman joins a man who already has assets, family obligations, and estate plans in motion, the risk of being silently left out is real. And when she does not ask what her place is in that plan, she is left to guess. Over time, guessing turns into anxiety. That anxiety becomes withdrawal. And eventually, both people end up resenting the other, for entirely different reasons. He might resent being questioned after years of providing. She might resent giving everything without ever being offered security. Both feel misunderstood. And both are right, because neither of them ever truly spoke their truth in the first place.

The solution is not dramatic. It does not require confrontation. It begins with the willingness to ask honest questions early. Where do I stand? What will happen if you die? If I contribute to this home, how will that be acknowledged? If we grow together, will my sacrifices matter? These are not selfish questions. They are the ones that create structure. Without them, there is only uncertainty disguised as peace. And sooner or later, uncertainty makes itself heard.

4. The unspoken pain of being temporary in someone else's permanent life

There is a particular kind of loneliness that settles in when you begin to realize you are building your daily life inside someone else's permanent structure. He may not say it. He may not even realize it. But everything around you quietly reminds you that this space was shaped without your input, and there has been no clear invitation for you to reshape any of it.

You begin to learn the boundaries without anyone needing to point them out. You learn that some traditions are untouchable. That certain rooms, memories, or decisions are off-limits. You sense that some topics make him uncomfortable. You avoid asking. You get used to not knowing where you stand. And you adjust. You begin to call things "his," not "ours." His house. His plans. His legacy. The language starts as a habit, but slowly it becomes the truth.

This kind of emotional limbo wears on you over time. You may still love him. You may still care deeply for the life you share. But part of you starts to hold back. You no longer offer ideas as freely. You no longer plan far into the future. You hesitate before making suggestions. You stop imagining that this story is fully yours. You begin to protect your own heart from feeling attached to something that could one day remind you it was never yours to begin with. This is not about ownership in the legal sense. It is about being given space to leave a mark. It is about knowing that your presence is not just welcomed, but needed. That your effort is not just accepted, but remembered. That you are not a quiet guest in a chapter you didn't write, but a co-creator of everything being built now.

When that assurance never comes, a woman begins to retreat emotionally. Sometimes it's slow. Sometimes she doesn't even realize it's happening. But the feeling that she is temporary makes it hard to give herself fully. And over time, the relationship feels less like a home and more like a lease. People don't talk about this often. Because to others, the relationship looks stable. It looks functional. There is no drama. No fights. The bills are paid. The home is kept. From the outside, everything seems fine. But inside, she is shrinking. Not because she is weak, but because she does not want to fight for a space she should already have.

There is a cost to emotional invisibility. And it is one many women pay quietly for years before they realize what they've lost.

The cure is not possession. It is partnership. It is the difference between being allowed to live in a life and being invited to shape it. When a woman feels that her role is secure, her heart can settle. Her voice gets stronger. Her contributions become confident. And the relationship deepens in ways no legal document alone can offer. No one wants to be a placeholder. Everyone wants to matter. If a relationship cannot offer that at its core, no surface-level gestures will ever make it feel like home.

There is a delicate balance that arises when a man comes into a relationship with something to protect. He may have worked hard for what he has. He may carry the responsibility of family property passed down through generations. He may feel a sense of duty to keep certain things untouched, reserved for his children or for the legacy he believes he is meant to preserve.

There is nothing wrong with that. In fact, protecting your children's future is often a sign of deep love. Wanting to honor the effort of parents who left something behind is understandable. But too often, this commitment to legacy turns into something else. Without realizing it, a man can begin to draw invisible lines that divide the life he shares with his partner from the life he feels he still owns alone.

These lines are rarely announced. They are not written on paper or spoken aloud. They show up in how decisions are made, in how things are framed. They show up when the house is always called "mine," when financial matters are kept behind a curtain, or when her input is quietly dismissed with the reasoning that "this was always meant for the kids."

What gets overlooked is the emotional consequence of this stance. When one person is asked to invest time, care, and presence into a life that already has boundaries she cannot cross, she begins to feel like a service provider. Not a partner. She may be expected to maintain the property, host the family, support the household, and raise children who are not hers biologically, while being told directly or indirectly that none of it will ever belong to her. That is exclusion dressed up as responsibility.

The fairness being sought here is not about taking something away from the children. It is about creating a structure where the woman helping sustain the life also gets to feel secure in it. A prenup can reflect that balance. So can a will. So can shared ownership agreements or repayment clauses. These tools exist not to strip anyone of what matters to them, but to acknowledge everyone who is contributing to what has become shared.

There is a misconception that any woman who questions the structure of legacy must be looking to take. But sometimes, she may just be looking to understand. She is looking for assurance that she is not a caretaker of someone else's empire with nothing to call her own. She is not asking to override history. She is asking to be included in the story now being written. Respecting a legacy and including a partner are not mutually exclusive. You can prepare your children for the future and still show your partner that she matters. The hard part is being willing to talk about it. Not with suspicion. Not with fear. But with maturity.

A woman who feels protected is not a threat to anyone's inheritance. She is someone who will give more freely, love more openly, and remain more rooted in the life you share, because she knows she is not standing on ground that will be pulled out from under her. That is what most women are asking for. Not entitlement. Just acknowledgment. Not control. Just clarity.

6. You don't want what's his, but you do want to belong

There is a misunderstanding that surrounds women in relationships where one partner holds most of the financial power. People assume the woman must be there for gain. That she is calculating. That she wants access. But often, the reality is the opposite. Many women in these relationships are not asking for someone else's assets. They are not trying to claim property they didn't buy or control decisions they didn't make. What they want, more than anything, is to feel like they belong in the life they are helping maintain. Belonging is not the same as ownership. It is about presence being recognized and integrated, not simply accommodated.

It becomes emotionally exhausting to live in a space where every part of the life you're supporting is still seen as someone else's domain. The man might not say anything directly. In fact, he might think he is being generous. He may see himself as giving access, as offering stability. But access is not the same as invitation. And stability is not the same as inclusion. Over time, a woman in this position starts to adjust her behavior. She begins to feel hesitant about making decisions. She starts to withdraw from things she initially wanted to invest in. She holds her opinions more quietly, not because she lacks thoughts or instincts, but because she no longer feels she has the right to shape anything around her.

That kind of emotional withdrawal doesn't happen overnight. It is a slow, quiet erosion. It often begins with practical things - whether she can decorate a room, whether she can speak up in front of his children, whether her name is listed on shared assets. But it always leads to deeper questions. Am I here as a partner, or just as support? Is this a shared life, or just one I've been allowed to live in?

Belonging is not about financial entitlement. It is about knowing that your existence is not conditional. That your presence is not being tolerated, but valued. That you are not replaceable, not just appreciated when it's convenient, but considered at every level of decision-making, because your role is seen as central.

There is dignity in being able to say, "I am part of this," without having to explain or justify it. For that to happen, a relationship must offer more than comfort. It must offer access to real partnership. Not in name, but in structure.

When a woman says she wants to feel like this life is hers too, she is not asking to strip anyone of what they've earned. She is asking to be visible in what she is still contributing to. And if her partner cannot recognize that difference, then the relationship is no longer built on love, but on a quiet imbalance that will eventually tip.

Belonging should not be earned through silence. It should be acknowledged through action. Especially in relationships where one person came in with more, it matters that the person who came in later is not made to feel like they're always standing at the edge of something that looks like theirs but never quite is.

7. The role of stepchildren, family history, and whose memories matter

If you're marrying someone with children from a previous relationship, you are not just joining a man. You are stepping into an entire emotional ecosystem. And whether people say it out loud or not, there are rules. There are loyalties. There are memories that have been sealed shut, and you are expected to walk around them without making too much noise.

Let's be honest. Blending families is not a neutral experience. There are birthdays where you don't know where to stand. Traditions you didn't create but are somehow expected to carry. Family photos that tell a story you're not in, but now live with. It is not just about adjusting, but about walking into a world that sometimes keeps you at the edge of the circle, even as you do everything to earn a place inside it.

The children didn't ask for any of this. Some of them may be kind. Some may be indifferent. Some may keep their distance. All of that is normal. But what makes it hard is when your partner doesn't see what this experience is doing to you. When he assumes that because you're strong, you're fine. When he doesn't recognize that loving someone else's children is generous work, and even when it's given freely, it still deserves acknowledgment.

You might cook for them, shop for them, show up at their events, and even carry their emotions during hard seasons. But if you bring up legal plans, or ask questions about how assets will be shared, suddenly the room gets cold. Suddenly, you're accused of not understanding "family." Suddenly, the same people who expect your unconditional support start reminding you where the boundaries are.

It's not just about the money. It's about the message. When you are asked to pour your time, energy, and care into someone else's children, you should be able to speak openly about what happens next. You should be able to say, "If I'm part of this family, then what does that actually mean?" without being made to feel like you're stepping out of line. You don't want to erase their mother. You don't want to take anyone's place. You just want to know that the work you're doing matters. That the love you're giving counts. That the years you're investing will not disappear the moment something changes.

If the family you support every day can still remind you that "this isn't really yours," then no amount of effort will make you feel secure. And if the man you're with lets that happen, even without meaning to, then the imbalance is not just emotional. It's structural.

This is why legal conversations matter. This is why financial planning should not be a secret. Because when things are left to assumptions, people get hurt. If you're being treated like family in daily life, but like an outsider when it comes to legacy, something is off. And sooner or later, that imbalance will come to the surface. If your memories are being built inside a life where your name is always left out of the plan, then yes, you love him. Yes, you may even love the children. But the truth is, you are still waiting to be chosen in a way that cannot be quietly undone.

8. Why emotional and financial security must go hand in hand

Let's not pretend that love alone is enough to keep someone safe. You can be cherished. You can be adored. You can be given affection, attention, and all the right words, but if you're still uncertain about where you stand financially, something inside you will always be unsettled. There are women who know they're loved, but still wake up in a house they don't feel safe in. Not because of physical danger, but because they know that if something happened tomorrow, an illness, a death, a divorce; they don't know what would be left for them. Their entire life is built around a man's structure, but their name isn't on the paperwork. They care for the home, manage the schedules, hold the emotional labor, but in legal terms, they are invisible.

You can't relax in love when you're walking on ground that might not hold you. You can't give your best when you're unsure whether you have a place in the future you're helping build. You can't keep pouring energy into something when you know it could all vanish with one signature or one decision made without you. That kind of instability changes people. It makes them second-guess their instincts. It makes them shrink when they should speak. It keeps them from making long-term plans because nothing feels secure enough to build on. You start thinking small just to stay safe. You stop dreaming because you're too busy preparing for what happens if things fall apart.

And what's worse is that often, when women try to bring this up, they're told they're being paranoid. Or ungrateful. Or that talking about money is cold. But it's not cold to want structure. It's not selfish to want protection. It's wise to ask, "What happens if I stay and give my life to this, what happens to me in the end?"

You need both. You need emotional safety and financial security. You need the love that makes you feel seen and the legal foundation that proves you're not replaceable. It's not a sign of mistrust to want your future to be clear. It's a sign that you respect yourself enough not to gamble everything on promises that can disappear when people change or life gets hard.

This is not about being cynical. It's about being clear. When you are secure on every level, emotionally, financially, legally, you show up differently in your relationship. You are not constantly calculating risk. You are not secretly preparing for impact. You are able to give with openness, because you know you are not giving into a system that could one day forget you were ever there. You deserve to feel safe. Not just in his arms, but on paper. Not just in what he says, but in what he's built to protect you.

9. The truth about resentment and why it doesn't come all at once

Resentment does not walk in through the front door. It sneaks in quietly, wearing the face of patience. It shows up when you've convinced yourself that small sacrifices don't matter. It builds slowly when you keep pushing your needs aside and telling yourself you're doing it for love. And before you know it, something that felt like devotion starts to taste like regret.

You may not realize it's happening at first. You think you're just tired. You think you're being mature. You let things go because you believe that's what a good partner does. But inside, you are starting to count. You count the times you said yes when you wanted to say no. You count the hours you gave, the plans you postponed, the pieces of yourself you slowly put in a drawer just to keep the peace. And then something small happens. He buys something without talking to you. He calls it "his house" in front of someone else. He changes the will and doesn't mention it. And suddenly you feel something sharp inside you. It's not anger. It's not rage. It's the realization that you've been waiting. Waiting for your turn. Waiting to be considered. Waiting to be more than a supporting role in a life you keep helping carry.

This is how resentment grows. Not through big betrayals, but through the slow denial of your voice. Through the unspoken agreement that you'll just go along with whatever has already been decided. Through the pressure to stay silent, be supportive, and trust that love is enough.

But love without structure eventually asks too much. It asks you to forget what you need. It asks you to accept uncertainty as stability. It asks you to settle for gestures instead of commitment. And over time, even the kindest woman becomes resentful when her value is not recognized with action. Resentment is not the problem. It's the signal, the evidence that something inside you is tired of pretending that this arrangement is fair. It's what rises up when you've tried to be understanding for too long and now realize that no one ever stopped to understand you.

It's tempting to bury it. To tell yourself that you should be grateful. That others have it worse. That he means well. But suppression does not turn into peace. It turns into disconnection. And that disconnection will eventually pull you so far out of the relationship that nothing can reach you anymore.

If you feel resentment growing, listen to it. Not because you want to fight, but because you want to stay connected. Because speaking now is better than drifting for years and realizing too late that you disappeared from your own life while trying to preserve someone else's. The truth is simple. If you have to silence your needs to keep love intact, then the love was never stable to begin with. And no amount of good intentions can undo the weight of feeling invisible in the life you show up for every day.

10. The question that haunts so many women: what happens to me if he dies?

This is not the kind of question most women ask out loud. At least, not at first. It sounds cold. It sounds like the kind of thing people bring up only after trust has already been broken. But the truth is, many women in long-term relationships are thinking about it quietly, often every day. They love the man. They're not trying to take what isn't theirs. They're not planning for failure. They're just doing the math in their minds while folding laundry or walking past the office where the financial decisions are made. And the question follows them like a shadow. If something happens to him, what happens to me?

There is one woman I remember clearly. She had been married for twelve years. Her husband had two adult children from a previous relationship, both in their thirties. When they got married, he already owned two properties and had a growing business. Clara had been working in a nonprofit at the time. She left her job a year into the marriage to help care for his aging mother and later took over the admin for his business when the office manager left. She did not complain once during the entire conversation. But you could feel the fatigue under her words. She said things like, "I just want clarity" and "I'm not trying to take anything from his kids." Her concern was mere theory. Her husband had recently recovered from a serious heart scare. That was when she realized she didn't know what the plan was. Not because he was hiding anything. But because they had never talked about it. She had trusted that her role spoke for itself.

When she asked him what would happen to the house if he passed, he told her not to worry. That everything was "in the trust." But he didn't explain what that meant. He didn't say who was in the trust. He didn't ask if she had any questions.

She helped maintain the house, take care of his health, his business, and his mother's final years, but the truth was she had no legal claim to the property, the assets, or the retirement accounts. His adult children didn't dislike her, but they didn't consider her family either. And when she looked at the situation clearly, she realized that she could lose the man and the home in the same month, with nothing left but memories. Its not rare. Women all over the world are giving their time, care, and effort into lives they do not own. And they're told that love should be enough. But love without a plan is not security. It is risk wrapped in comfort. When the plan is not clear, grief becomes chaotic. Love turns into suspicion. Families split into sides. And the person who gave everything is left trying to prove they mattered. You don't ask this question because you're greedy. You ask it because you've built your life on the assumption that you are not temporary. And if the answer to that question is uncertain, then something has to change before it's too late.

What happens to me if he dies? If you don't know the answer, and if no one's ever taken the time to walk you through it, then it's time to stop pretending that love alone is enough.

TWO

What Fair Really Looks Like

Fairness is a word people love to use but rarely agree on. It sounds good in conversation and looks mature in legal documents. It's the term we reach for when we want to sound reasonable. But in real relationships, fairness is not always easy to recognize, especially when love, labor, and legacy all show up in the same space.

What one person sees as generous, another might experience as barely enough. What feels protective to one may feel exclusionary to the other. The problem isn't that people want unfair arrangements. It's that they often have no shared definition of what fairness means in the first place.

Now let us build that definition from real-life experience. From the voices of women who gave up years of work to raise children. From men who came into marriages with property and didn't know how to share it without losing control. From couples who tried to protect themselves and ended up hurting each other instead. Fairness is not just about splitting numbers down the middle. It's about being seen. It's about recognizing labor that isn't always paid. It's about protecting the person beside you without leaving them unprotected when you are no longer there.

When we talk about a fair prenup, we are not just talking about percentages. We are talking about power. About care. About who gets to feel safe and who is left wondering what they're worth after the vows have been said. This is where that conversation begins.

1. When she gives up her career, what is that truly worth?

There are women who leave their jobs to support a relationship, and when they do, they are often told it is a shared sacrifice. That the family will benefit. That the partnership will grow stronger. And sometimes that is true.

But what happens when the relationship ends, or when the man passes away, or when the business she helped support with her unpaid labor thrives without her name on anything?

The answer is often silence.

There was this lady who had been a corporate events manager in her early thirties, driven, and earning well. Then she married a man who owned three construction companies. They agreed that she would leave her job and help him manage the backend of the businesses. Payroll, scheduling, admin, supplier relationships. She did it all from home, unofficially. She never asked for a salary. She saw herself as part of the team. She saw it as theirs. Over time, she took over managing the household too. Appointments, bills, school runs. They had two children together, and she raised them full-time while his empire kept expanding. His name was on everything. The business, the house, the retirement accounts. Hers was on the kids' school forms and the grocery list.

When he died unexpectedly at fifty-six, she was left with almost nothing. The business passed to his brother, who had a silent stake in the company. The house was willed to his children from a previous marriage. She was not even listed as a beneficiary on the life insurance policy.

She told me she didn't cry the day she got the news from the lawyer. She just stood there thinking about the years, in the disbelief that a life she helped keep afloat could erase her this quickly. What a prenup could have done in her case wasn't to strip him of his business or force an unnatural split of assets. It could have made her contributions visible. It could have set clear terms. It could have protected her without harming what he wanted to pass on to his children. But the conversation never happened. Because she trusted love. Because she didn't want to seem like she was thinking about money. Because he said, "Don't worry, I've got it covered."

And then he was gone. And she wasn't covered. Not emotionally. Not financially. Not legally.

A woman's decision to pause or walk away from her career should never be taken lightly. And it should never be treated like a favor she's doing for her partner. It's an investment. And like all real investments, it comes with risk. A fair prenup is not just about who owns what now. It's about who gave up what along the way.

2. Why emotional labor and caregiving must be acknowledged

Some forms of work come with paychecks, performance reviews, titles, and promotions. Others come with nothing but expectation. No one signs a contract to keep the household emotionally balanced. No one gets paid for remembering birthdays, organizing family events, anticipating moods, softening tension, or holding space for everyone else's needs before their own. But that work is real. It's not invisible because it can't be seen. It's invisible because we have not been taught to count it.

I once worked with a couple where the husband ran a successful architecture firm. His life was booked in calendar blocks and project milestones. His wife, after their second child, left her job in publishing. At first, the plan was temporary. A year at home. Then back to work. But their daughter had developmental delays. Yvonne stayed. There was always a reason. A school adjustment. A therapy schedule. A parent who needed extra care.

She wasn't idle. She ran the home like a quiet machine. She remembered who needed what and when. She managed emotional weather, not just logistics. If someone was upset, she noticed before anyone else did. If a teacher called, she was the one who responded. If the family needed to function, she was the one who made it happen. The strain came years later when they sat down to talk about estate planning. Martin, with no malice, suggested the house would go to the children, the retirement plan was set, and most of his business assets were going into a trust. Yvonne listened quietly. Then she asked, "Where do I fit in?"

He looked confused. He said, "You'll always be taken care of."

She didn't need to be taken care of. She needed to be seen.

In that moment, every unpaid hour, every night spent worrying about everyone else, every day she organized her identity around other people's needs, all of it felt like it had vanished into air. Because when the real planning began, her role had no place on the page.

That is what happens when emotional labor is never acknowledged. You don't just feel tired. You feel replaceable. You feel erased. There is no app that measures what it costs to keep a household emotionally stable. There is no resume line for walking someone through illness, for calming your partner after a business loss, for helping your stepchild trust again. But just because you can't list it doesn't mean it doesn't shape lives. And just because you didn't ask for recognition doesn't mean you didn't deserve it.

In relationships where one person becomes the emotional core, fairness cannot be measured in money alone. It has to include the care, the presence, and the long stretches of time when someone held up an entire world without ever asking to be thanked.

A prenup cannot assign a dollar amount to empathy. But it can recognize that support is not free. That caregiving builds stability. That unpaid labor is part of what makes wealth and success possible in the first place. If emotional work made the relationship possible, it should not be forgotten when the legal plans begin.

3. Sacrificing your goals to support someone else's dream

Every couple says they're building a life together. But if you look closely, you'll sometimes find that only one person is actually building while the other is holding everything up behind the scenes. Not by accident. By design. One person grows, while the other makes room for that growth. And most of the time, it's the woman who does the rearranging.

It starts with what feels like a mutual decision. You agree that his career has more earning potential. That your job can be paused for now. That he needs to travel, and someone needs to be home more often. That it just makes sense, given the timing. But one year turns into three. Then five. Then a decade. And while he climbs the ladder, you are managing the everyday details that allow that climb to happen smoothly. You plan the moves. You pack the boxes. You do the emotional cleanup after each transition. You explain the changes to the kids. You settle into each new version of his dream.

Most women do all of this willingly. Not because they don't have ambitions of their own, but because they love the person they're with. And when you love someone, you want to see them win. You don't ask for recognition every step of the way. You give what's needed, and you expect that, one day, it will all balance out. But time passes. It may have felt like a shared dream but then it starts to look like a very lopsided arrangement.

I remember a woman had been accepted into a graduate program for clinical psychology. It was a dream she'd held onto since college. The same month she got the letter, her husband was offered a promotion that required them to relocate across the country. They sat down, and she told him she would defer. Just one year. Let him get settled. Let their two young kids adjust. Then she would apply again.

One year turned into four. His role expanded. Their life got busier. And every time she brought up her plans, he responded with something that sounded supportive on the surface but pushed the timeline further. "This year's too hectic." "Let's wait until the kids are a little older." "Why don't you look into something part-time?"

She never applied again.

When they came in to draft a prenup, he was confused when she asked to include language about spousal support and deferred career compensation. He said, "We've always shared everything. Why would we need that?" And she looked at me and said, "Because I'm tired of sharing quietly and receiving nothing concrete in return." Supporting someone's dream is not a problem. But giving up your own dream with no roadmap for what that means legally or financially? That creates a quiet erosion that no amount of affection can fix.

Fairness means honoring what was lost. It means not expecting someone to shrink themselves without building in the protection they need to stand on their own if everything changes. It means understanding that just because a decision was made with love doesn't mean it should leave one person with nothing to show for years of sacrifice. If one person's dream gets built on the back of another's pause, then the plan must reflect that. Not in vague promises. Not in "we'll figure it out." But in writing. In clear terms. In mutual respect. Because love may inspire sacrifice. But fairness is what turns that sacrifice into something that lasts.

4. Investing time and effort without legal recognition

There is a difference between helping someone and being part of something. Helping feels like something temporary, something optional, something that can be taken for granted. Being part of something means you have a role. A place. A right to be seen. And for too many women in long-term relationships, the work they do lives in that blurry space between the two.

You show up. You organize. You rearrange your life to support theirs. You pour your energy into daily tasks that keep everything running smoothly. You build schedules. You create systems. You take things off his plate so he can focus on the bigger picture. But somewhere in the middle of all that effort, you start to notice something.

There is no record of what you do. No contract. No recognition on paper. No security. If someone were to look at the financial documents, the property titles, the business filings, or the long-term plans, they would not see your name. They would see his. This is what happens when time and labor are treated as personal contributions instead of legal value. It sounds noble. It looks loving. But it leaves you vulnerable.

Many women make the mistake of thinking that because something feels shared, it will eventually be acknowledged as such. That because you were there through the busy seasons, because you made things easier, because you gave freely, the reward will come. But rewards are not automatic. They are built into structure. And if no structure exists, the effort you gave becomes invisible the moment someone chooses not to see it.

This is not about demanding compensation for every supportive act. It is about protecting the truth of your contribution. If the relationship ends, whether by death or divorce, and your name is not on anything, the legal system will not assume you were a partner. It will look at the paper. It will look at the titles. It will look at the assets and decide whether you are entitled to something based on what was legally established, not emotionally earned.

That is why these conversations are critical. To protect your heart, time, and the years you spent showing up in ways that made everything possible for the other person and the family to succeed. You cannot go back and rewrite the beginning. But you can take responsibility for what happens next. And you can choose not to pour your energy into a life where your role is treated as temporary, even when you are showing up like someone who plans to stay.

5. When financial silence feels like control, not privacy

There are people who believe that money should never be discussed in a relationship. That it is private. That love should not have to pass through spreadsheets and estate plans to be real. But in practice, what starts as privacy often becomes silence. And what begins as discretion often becomes control.

Not everyone who avoids financial conversations is being secretive on purpose. Some were raised to think money talk is rude. Others feel ashamed of their past choices or unsure about how to start. But no matter the reason, when one partner has more power over the finances and the other is left in the dark, the balance of the relationship starts to shift.

The one who knows begins to make decisions. The one who does not begins to guess.

You feel it when you ask about the budget and get vague answers. You feel it when major purchases are made without your input. You feel it when you realize that everything is structured around his name, his plan, his future.

This is not about needing control over everything. It is about wanting to live in a life that includes you at every level. It is about not having to ask for access to information that directly affects your safety and security.

When your partner holds all the information and insists that you just trust them, you start to wonder whether this is still a partnership or if you are just along for the ride. And no matter how much love you feel in other parts of the relationship, the silence starts to grow into something heavier. You begin to monitor your spending more carefully, not because he asked you to, but because you do not want to cross an invisible line. You stop asking questions because the answers are always uncomfortable. You begin to adapt to a life you do not fully understand.

This is what financial silence does. It does not keep peace. It creates distance. And that distance, once it grows large enough, is very hard to come back from. If the plan includes you, you should know what it is. If the house is shared, you should understand how it is protected. If the future is being planned, you should be in the room.

A fair prenup does not just protect assets. It creates space for clarity. It sets the expectation that both partners deserve full understanding, even if the finances are not split evenly. Because this is not about equality of numbers. It is about equality of respect. When someone tells you they just do not want to talk about money, ask yourself why. Is it about discomfort? Or is it about keeping control? Privacy has its place. But when you are building a life together, information is not a luxury. It is the ground you walk on. And you cannot build anything stable when only one person can see the floor plan.

6. Why love doesn't erase the need for structure

It is one of the biggest lies people tell themselves in relationships. That love will be enough. That deep connection can replace legal clarity. That if someone truly loves you, they will do right by you no matter what.

But love is not structure. It is not a legal plan. It is not a replacement for clear decisions. Love is an emotion. Powerful, beautiful, necessary, but not always predictable. It can rise and fall. It can be shaped by time, by stress, by change, and even by fear. Which is why building a life on love alone is not enough.

Structure is what remains when feelings shift. It is what protects both people from the impact of uncertainty. It is what says, even if we go through hard seasons, you are not left behind. Even if the marriage changes, you are not discarded. Even if death or illness or conflict shows up, there is something in place that reflects what we agreed on when we were at our best.

Too many people avoid this truth because they are afraid of what it means. They think structure means distrust. That if you ask for a prenup, you are assuming the worst. But asking for structure is not about expecting failure. It is about honoring the reality that life is full of unknowns. And it is about making decisions while you still care deeply, not after something has gone wrong.

The couples who last are not the ones who avoid these conversations. They are the ones who face them early. Who say clearly, this is what I have. This is what I want to protect. This is what I want to share. This is how I see fairness. And then they listen. Not just to be polite, but to understand. Because understanding is the root of trust. Not emotion alone.

A fair prenup is not an escape plan. It is a blueprint. It lays out what matters. It acknowledges what has come before and what both people are bringing to the table. And it sets the stage for what they hope to build together. It does not kill romance. It gives romance a stable home.

If you are afraid to talk about structure because you think it will ruin the love, you are already building on shaky ground. Real love is strong enough to be practical. It is not scared of detail, or threatened by boundaries. It knows that safety does not come from words. It comes from the work of making sure both people are truly protected.

7. When fear of asking keeps you outside the plan

There are many reasons people stay silent. Some are afraid of seeming greedy. Others do not want to appear ungrateful. Many just do not know how to start the conversation. They worry that bringing up money or ownership or legal plans will make them look suspicious or selfish, so they wait. They try to be patient. They try to prove they are trustworthy by not asking too many questions.You end up living inside someone else's plan without ever knowing what the terms are. You move forward in a life that has already been designed, but not with you in mind. And because you never asked to be part of the decision-making, you are not included when the real decisions are made.

It is easy to tell yourself that love will make up for it. That loyalty will be rewarded. That showing how undemanding you are will earn you a place at the table. But relationships are not built on quietness, but on participation. And you cannot participate fully in something you are afraid to question.

It is not disrespectful to want to know what happens if things change. It is not disloyal to ask what part of the future is yours. It is not a betrayal to say, I am building this life with you, and I want to be protected inside of it. If you wait until things go wrong to speak, it may be too late. If you wait until someone else brings it up, they may never do it. And if you keep convincing yourself that asking for clarity will ruin the peace, you are living in a peace that depends on your silence. That is not stability. That is survival.

A fair prenup gives you the right to ask. It says your voice matters. It says your future matters. It says you are not afraid to be honest about the life you are building, even if that honesty feels uncomfortable in the moment. If you are asking, it means you want to be treated like a full partner. And if the person you are with cannot handle that, the problem is not your question. The problem is the imbalance that your question just exposed.

8. Why protecting your future does not mean planning for failure

It is a mistake people often make. They hear the word prenup and they think divorce. They hear the idea of legal protection and they think distrust. They assume that if you plan for what happens in the worst-case scenario, you must be expecting things to fall apart.

But planning is not the same as predicting. Protection is not the same as pessimism. It is possible to be deeply in love and still want to be prepared. It is possible to trust someone and still want your own safety. You do not wear a seatbelt because you expect to crash. You wear it because you understand that life can be unpredictable, and preparation is part of responsibility.

The truth is that many of the strongest relationships are not the ones built on blind hope. They are built on honesty. On clarity. On the ability to sit down together and say, this is what I want to protect, and this is what I want to give, and this is how we make sure that no matter what happens, neither of us will walk away broken or bitter. There is no shame in wanting to protect yourself. There is no weakness in making sure your years of care, your work, your loyalty, your time, and your presence are honored not just with affection but with real structure.

Too many women enter marriages assuming that love will shield them from loss. They believe that if they are good enough, giving enough, supportive enough, that nothing bad will happen. But things happen. People die. People change. Businesses shift. Families grow tense. And if you have no plan in place when that happens, your life can unravel quickly. A fair prenup is not a prediction of disaster. It is a confirmation of value. It says, I care about you so much that I am willing to have the hard conversations now, so we both know we are safe. So that if something changes, we are not enemies. We are two people who planned well. You can be romantic and still be wise. You can believe in the best and still prepare for the unexpected. Love is not weakened by structure. If anything, it grows stronger when both people feel protected inside it.

9. If it's just his name on everything, is it still your life?

You ever look around and realize you're living in a house that doesn't feel like it belongs to you? Because everything, the deed, the bank accounts, the passwords, the retirement plans, has someone else's name on it. And that someone isn't you.

And the thing is, it doesn't hit you all at once. It starts as a passing thought, something you brush off because it feels too small to matter. But that is exactly how the danger shows up. Quietly. Slowly. In the background of a life you're fully present in but barely documented in.

It might not seem like a big deal at first. Maybe you moved in after the house was already bought. Maybe the accounts were already set up. Maybe the business was already running before you got involved. So you tell yourself it's fine. You're part of it now. That's what matters.

But then time passes. Years go by. You're contributing in ways no one sees. You're making his life easier. You're folding your schedule around his. You're showing up every single day. And one morning, you realize that if someone looked at the paperwork, the actual legal stuff that defines ownership and protection, they wouldn't see your name anywhere. Not on the house. Not on the business. Not on the plan for what happens if something goes wrong. You love this person. You've built a life around them. But if your name isn't on anything, then whose life are you really living?

This is the kind of thing that creeps up on you. Nobody tells you that the absence of your name means the absence of security. But it does. Because if something changes; he gets sick, he passes away, the relationship ends, you could lose everything you've helped sustain without a single right to it. And let's be honest, it feels bad. Because you want to know that the life you're building with someone isn't just happening around you. You want to know that you are in it, fully. Not just emotionally. Legally. Practically. Tangibly.

And that is exactly where the danger sits. Ownership isn't about greed or suspicion. It is about visibility. It is about making sure the life you're giving yourself to actually acknowledges you. When you disappear from the paperwork, you disappear from the protection. And that is not a small thing. That is how people end up with nothing after giving everything.

When we talk about prenups being fair, this is what we mean. A prenup is not just a safety net. It is a way to make sure your name is part of the story. That your time, your energy, your presence, and your partnership are all backed up by structure. Not just love. Not just vibes. Actual structure. So if you've ever caught yourself saying "his house," or "his business," or "his retirement," ask yourself why. Ask yourself how that happened. And more importantly, ask yourself what you want to do about it.

10. Love is not a financial plan

Let's be real about something most people don't like to say boldly. Just because someone loves you doesn't mean they've built a future that includes you. And love, on its own, is not a plan. It's not a legal safety net. It's not a financial roadmap. It doesn't protect your name, your time, your work, or your sacrifices. People hear that and get defensive. They'll say, "But we love each other. We're not planning to break up." And yes, that's beautiful. But life doesn't care if you're in love. Life brings illness. Accidents. Job losses. Unexpected deaths. Changes you didn't see coming. And when those things show up, love cannot substitute for structure.

When couples avoid the money talk because they think it'll ruin the romance, what they're really doing is pushing discomfort down the road. They believe silence equals peace. But silence is just delay. Eventually, that conversation comes back around. Only by then, the stakes are higher and the tone is different.

You want to know what's actually romantic? Security. Knowing that the person you're with thought ahead. That they didn't just say they loved you, they created a plan that reflects that love in action. That they were willing to sit with the uncomfortable questions and come up with real answers, not just sweet words. Because the hard truth is that if your partner refuses to talk about money, refuses to include your name in anything official, and tells you that love should be enough, they're not protecting the relationship. They're protecting themselves. They're hoping the topic never comes up because the way things are right now works for them. And that silence? It's costing you. You cannot afford to confuse love with planning. Love is the feeling. Planning is the action. You deserve both.

THREE

The New Prenup Conversation

Let's talk about *everything you were afraid to ask and everything no one ever taught you to say*. You're in love, you're moving toward forever, and you start asking yourself: What happens if this doesn't go the way we hope? What if I give my whole self to this life and end up with nothing to show for it? What if everything I helped build ends up in someone else's name? Somehow, you push it away because you're afraid of sounding selfish. You don't want to mess up the moment. You think bringing up a prenup will make things weird. You convince yourself that if you love each other enough, you'll be fine.

Love does not replace a plan. You can have the deepest connection in the world and still find yourself completely unprotected when things get complicated. You can be loyal and still end up forgotten. You can be supportive and still be erased from the parts of the life that matter most.

If you've been afraid to ask, this chapter is for you. If you've been told that wanting a prenup makes you cold or calculating, this chapter will remind you that protecting yourself is not the same as planning to leave. And if you've been waiting for someone to bring it up first, this chapter will show you how to start the conversation with confidence and care.

1. Understanding what a prenup really means

A prenup is not just a document for rich people who don't trust each other. It is not some cold agreement meant to sit between you and the person you love. It is not a trap. It is not a warning. It is not an insult. What it really is, at its best, is a tool. It is a way to have hard conversations before life forces them on you. It is a way to be clear about what matters before things get complicated. It is a quiet kind of maturity that most people are too scared to talk about.

A prenup is just a written understanding. It puts structure around things that could one day feel uncertain. It gives both people a voice before pressure or pain shows up and distorts the story. And no, it doesn't mean you don't trust your partner. It means you're thinking clearly and responsibly. It means you're aware that people change, that circumstances shift, and that clarity is better than confusion, no matter how in love you are right now.

You are not heartless for wanting one, or cynical for asking for it. You are someone who understands that love needs more than emotion to survive. It needs a shared language. It needs honesty. It needs protection that works in both good seasons and bad ones.

The prenup conversation should not be about what you're afraid of losing. It should be about what you're building and how you're choosing to protect it with care and intention. When both people understand that, it stops feeling like a threat. It starts to feel like a partnership.

2. Starting the hard conversation without ruining the relationship

The hardest part is usually just saying it out loud. You can sit with the thought for weeks, maybe months. You try to find the right time. You wait for the perfect moment. And it never really comes, because there is no perfect moment to say, I want to talk about a prenup. There is no soft landing for a conversation most people don't even know how to begin.

But the longer you wait, the heavier it gets. You start to walk on eggshells. You start to hold your breath. And eventually, the silence starts to feel more damaging than the conversation ever would have been. You do not need to lead with fear. You do not need to justify your feelings. You can just be honest. Say that you've been thinking about how to protect what both of you are building. Say that it matters to you that both people feel seen and safe. Say that you want to have a clear understanding so no one is left guessing down the line. What you are doing is not selfish. It is responsible. And if the person you love is committed to the same level of clarity, they may be surprised, they may have feelings, but they will hear you.

If they get angry, shut down, or make you feel small for bringing it up, that tells you something more important than any legal document could. It tells you how conflict might be handled in the relationship long-term.

3. When protection becomes quiet control

It starts out sounding like love. He wants to take care of everything. He says he doesn't want you to stress about money or legal stuff. You're his girl, he's got it covered. He'll pay for everything, manage everything, handle all the decisions. And maybe at first, it feels like a dream. Someone finally wants to take the weight off your shoulders. Someone who wants to give you rest, security, stability. What could possibly be wrong with that?

But slowly, you stop being included in things. You don't know how the finances work. You don't know what's in the accounts. You're not sure if your name is on anything. You start to feel unsure about what's yours, or what would happen if something ever changed. And when you ask, the answers don't feel like answers. They sound like, "Why are you worried about that," or "I already took care of it," or "You don't need to be thinking about that right now." That's when you feel the shift. It no longer feels like protection, but like you're on the outside of your own life.

The control doesn't always show up loud. Sometimes, it's just silence. Sometimes, it's just not being invited into the room. Not being shown the papers. Not being asked what you think. You don't realize how far out you are until something goes wrong and you have no access, no answers, and no say in the decisions that matter most.

A partner who wants to protect you also wants you informed. They want you to feel confident, not clueless. They want you to understand what's happening in your life, not depend on them blindly. Protection means watching each other's back; not keeping one person in the dark so the other can stay in charge. And listen, not every man who wants to "take care of things" has bad intentions. Sometimes, he really does think he's doing you a favor. But intention doesn't always match impact. If your world is being managed without your input, then it's not love you're experiencing, it's control, even if it's wrapped in luxury. That's why conversations about prenups matter. Because they force everyone to put things on the table. They take away the guessing. They invite both people to say what they want, what they need, and what they're afraid of. And if someone is uncomfortable having that conversation, you have to ask yourself why.

A fair relationship doesn't just make space for you to feel safe. It makes space for you to speak, to ask, to understand, and to have your hands on the wheel too. You don't have to be loud to take your place in the room. But you do have to be present. You have to be informed. And you have to know when love has become something that quietly holds you back while pretending to hold you close.

4. What must be written down and why feelings are not enough

A lot of people believe that if you love someone enough, the rest will fall into place. You don't need to put things in writing, you don't need to talk about ownership, and you definitely don't need to plan for anything going wrong. The love is there, so the protection will be too. Right?

But love is not a legal agreement. It's not a name on a deed. It's not an insurance policy. It's not a will. Love might make someone mean well, but it doesn't guarantee follow-through. People forget things. People change their minds. People die without warning. People get scared and selfish. And when that happens, the only thing that stands between you and uncertainty is what's written down. You need more than vibes.

You need to know if your name is on the house. You need to know if there's life insurance and whether you're the beneficiary. You need to understand what happens to shared property if something goes wrong. If there are kids, you need to know how their future is being protected. If he owns a business, you need to know how that fits into the bigger picture. These things are not about greed. They're about being smart. They're about not waking up one day and realizing you've spent years building something that was never really yours.

You may love him. He may love you. But if his lawyer, his will, his financial advisor, and every document he's ever signed points to a future that leaves you out, then where does that love show up when it matters most? Putting things in writing is not cold. It only shows that what you have today is important enough to protect for tomorrow. It's deciding, together, that you're not just hoping for the best, you're actually preparing for it.

And if the person you're with refuses to put anything in writing, even after you've explained why it matters to you, you have to take a step back. Because anyone who loves you should want you to feel secure. Anyone who says they care should be willing to make sure that care isn't just a feeling. It's a fact. You deserve to know the plan. You deserve to help shape it. And you deserve more than promises. You deserve proof.

5. Creating a Fair Agreement that honors Love and Clarity

A prenup should not feel like one person winning and the other person losing. It should not feel like someone taking all the power while the other person gets nothing but a signature. If it feels like that, then it is not a fair prenup. It is a warning sign dressed up in legal language.

The truth is, a fair prenup does not start with fear. It starts with love. Not just emotional love, but real, practical, I-want-you-to-be-safe love. The kind that sees the future, not just the honeymoon. The kind that says, I care enough to make sure you will be okay, even if life takes us in a direction we did not expect.

Fairness in a prenup looks like understanding what your partner gave up to be with you. It looks like thinking about how to protect the time, care, work, and energy they are contributing to your shared life. It looks like making space for both of you to thrive, no matter who earns more or owns more.

This does not mean giving everything away. It does not mean pretending there is no risk. It means being honest about what you value, and being willing to protect that without making the other person feel small or disposable. It means saying, here is what matters to me, and here is what I am willing to do to protect you too. When done right, a prenup can be a beautiful thing. It says you thought ahead. It says you are not afraid to name your truth. It says you are showing up for your life with your eyes open and your heart steady.

It is not a wall between you. It is a foundation beneath you. It holds you both up. It lets you build with trust because the hard things are already spoken for. And when you know you are safe, when you know that even in the worst-case scenario you will still be treated with fairness and respect, you love more freely. You don't need to be naive to believe in love. You just need to be honest enough to build it wisely.

6. Building a Prenup that doesn't erase your Partner's dignity

There's this idea some people have, especially in heated conversations about money and divorce, that someone always has to walk away destroyed. That one person must end up broke, bitter, or embarrassed while the other one "wins." But dignity isn't something you should aim to take from someone, no matter how the relationship ends. A fair prenup doesn't just protect wealth. It protects humanity. And one of the best public examples of this is how MacKenzie Scott handled her divorce from Jeff Bezos.

Let's think about this. Jeff Bezos was, and still is, one of the richest men in the world. When he and MacKenzie divorced in 2019, some people braced for drama. They expected court battles. They expected someone to be humiliated and headlines to go wild with figures and blame.

That never happened.

MacKenzie walked away gracefully. She received about 4% of Amazon stock, which at the time was worth nearly thirty-eight billion dollars. But here's the part that matters more than the numbers. Jeff retained voting control over her shares. She chose not to drag out negotiations. She didn't try to take him down in the media. She didn't compete with his status. She simply took what was fair and allowed him to walk away with the identity he had built. Not as a man who had been defeated, but as someone who had been divorced with dignity.

MacKenzie Scott did help build Amazon from the ground up. She was there from the garage days, and was a part of the team before it became a trillion-dollar company. She could have claimed more. She could've demanded it. She had every legal and emotional reason to fight. But she chose fairness. She chose dignity. She walked away financially secure and emotionally intact, and she left him the same.

That's what a fair, well-thought-out prenup should aim to do.

It's not about giving everything away. It's about making sure that when two people go their separate ways, no one has to feel like they were erased. That even when love ends, respect stays in place. That both names come out of the process still standing. When you build a prenup with dignity in mind, you ask questions that go beyond assets. You ask, what would it look like for both of us to walk away proud of how we treated each other? What do I need to feel secure, and what does my partner need to feel honored? What can we do now to make sure that if life gets hard, we don't lose our character in the chaos?

Jeff Bezos remained the richest man in the world even after his divorce. That wasn't an accident, but the result of two people making conscious, calm, and respectful decisions. That's what it looks like when a prenup doesn't just protect your money, but also your dignity.

FOUR

Where the Line Really Is

Everyone talks about fairness like it's this clean idea. Like it's something you can measure exactly with the right tools and good intentions. But fairness gets complicated when feelings enter the room. When history shows up. When one person gave up years of their life and the other person says none of it counts because the house was in their name the whole time.

The truth is, not every love story is equal. Some people enter the relationship already holding the keys. Others show up trying to prove they're worthy of being there at all. And no matter how much love you start with, the balance of power will always show up if you're not paying attention.

There's a difference between protecting yourself and hiding behind legal walls. There's a difference between setting healthy boundaries and refusing to share the life you claim to be building together. And there's definitely a difference between someone who wants to be cared for and someone who is only there for what they can take.

Let's adress those lines. The ones people don't like to admit exist. The ones that separate healthy protection from quiet manipulation. The ones that help you tell the difference between a partner and a parasite. Between smart planning and subtle cruelty. Between a fair prenup and a weapon disguised as one.

We're going to look at the harder truths here. Why some women get labeled as gold diggers when all they did was ask for stability. Why sugar daddies exist and what the real problem is in those relationships. Why emotional safety can sometimes hide a deeper power imbalance that nobody talks about until it's too late.

This is the chapter that helps you sharpen your lens. Because when it comes to your future, your love, and your legacy, you need to know exactly where you stand. You need to be clear on what's fair, what's toxic, and what's just hiding behind money and romance to get what it wants.

1. The truth about gold diggers and why they are the exception not the norm

The word gold digger gets thrown around so easily it barely has weight anymore. A woman asks for a prenup and suddenly she is a gold digger. She mentions wanting security and people call her manipulative. She leaves a bad relationship and walks away with money and now she is a threat to every man who has ever made a dollar. But if you think of every woman as a gold digger, you are making a mistake. They are builders. They are protectors. They are women who gave up jobs, paused careers, raised children, and poured themselves into a life they thought they were part of.

It is easy to label someone a gold digger when you are trying to distract from the fact that they invested years into a relationship that left them with nothing in their name. It is easy to shame women for asking for security when nobody talks about the emotional, physical, and financial labor they carried every day. And yes, there are people who marry for money and never intend to contribute anything real. That exists. But those people are loud and obvious and rare. They are not the reason most women ask for fairness.

Asking for a prenup does not mean you are after someone's money. It means you are thinking ahead. It means you understand that love can be deep and still needs direction. It means you are not willing to live in someone else's life without a say in how that life works. That is not greed. That is emotional maturity.

Gold digger is a label people can use sometimes when they are not looking deeper. It is easier to point fingers than to face the fact that a woman asking for protection might actually need it. It is easier to assume she is plotting than to admit she might be responding to a power imbalance that was there all along.

Real relationships deserve more than suspicion. They deserve real conversations. They deserve legal clarity. And women who love deeply, give deeply, and stay through the hard seasons deserve more than a side-eye and a stereotype when they finally ask for something solid. If someone calls you a gold digger just for asking where your name fits in the future you are building, they are telling on themselves. They are telling you that their money matters more than your presence. They are telling you that your voice makes them uncomfortable. And most of all, they are telling you that they never expected to treat you like a partner in the first place.

2. Sugar daddies power imbalance and why age gaps are not always the problem

'Sugar daddy' is another term that gets tossed around so casually that people often forget there is a real story behind it. When we see a younger woman with an older man, the assumption is that she is there for money and he is there for her beauty and physique. Simple. Shallow. Mutually understood. But the reality behind those relationships is a lot more complex than most people admit.

Age gaps by themselves are not the issue. Plenty of couples with a ten or twenty year difference build strong, equal, and lasting relationships. The real issue is not age. It is power and how that power is used, or misused, when one person walks into the relationship already owning everything, knowing everything, deciding everything. And the other person is still trying to figure out who they are, what they want, and where they belong.

In most sugar relationships, the structure is transactional. One person brings lifestyle. The other brings attention. And as long as both people are honest about that, fine. But the problem shows up when people start calling it love without acknowledging what is being traded. Or worse, when the older partner uses their experience and money to shape the younger person's world without their input.

The imbalance shows up in times when she cannot speak up without being told she is lucky to be there. When she is made to feel small for having her own opinions. When her access to things is controlled. When her life becomes more about keeping the peace than actually having a say.

If a prenup ever enters this kind of situation, it is usually designed to protect the older, wealthier partner. But the question we need to start asking more often is who is protecting her. Not just from financial loss, but also emotional erasure. From a future she has no voice in. From being replaced the moment she stops being convenient. It is not wrong to love someone older. It is not wrong to fall for someone successful. But if the relationship is built in a way that one person always has the upper hand, then it is not love. It is leverage. And if that leverage shows up in silence, in paperwork, in what she is never allowed to ask for, then it is not a relationship. It is a contract she never got to write.

So no, age is not always the problem. But if age comes with a built-in power dynamic that never gets acknowledged, then the structure is already uneven. And you cannot build something fair on a foundation where only one person is allowed to stand tall.

3. What to do when love is used as a transaction

There is a kind of love that feels like a trade. You give something and get something back, not out of generosity, but out of expectation. You show up emotionally, physically, or financially, and in return you are offered a version of love that depends on how well you play your role. Maybe they never say it out loud, but you feel it. The silent exchange. The pressure to keep performing in order to keep being wanted. It happens more than most people admit. And it is not always about money. Sometimes the transaction is emotional. You provide stability. You carry their weight. You become their peace, their logic, their anchor. And in return, they give you just enough affection to keep you in place, but never enough to feel safe. In other cases, the transaction is more obvious. You get access to a lifestyle, and they get access to your body, your attention, your youth, your time. It can start off feeling mutual. Even exciting. But it slowly shifts when one person begins to feel owned instead of loved.

Love that feels like a transaction is not always toxic at first glance. It can look stable. It can feel secure. But over time, it becomes exhausting. Because you are constantly trying to earn your position. You are constantly measuring your value. And deep down, you know that if you ever stop giving, the whole thing might disappear.

So what do you do when love starts to feel like a deal you never signed up for? You name it and stop pretending it is romantic. You stop dressing it up as devotion. You admit that what you are experiencing is not a partnership. It is an exchange where one person always seems to have more power.

Then you ask yourself a harder question. What am I getting out of this, and is it worth the parts of me I am losing to stay here? No one wants to believe they are in a transactional relationship. But the moment you feel like you are no longer safe to rest, to speak, to grow, or to say no, you are not in love. You are in an arrangement. And those arrangements usually do not come with real protection. Because the moment you stop meeting expectations, the support disappears.

If you are going to build a life with someone, it cannot be based on trade. It has to be based on choice. On a commitment to each other's freedom, not just each other's usefulness. Otherwise, all you are doing is negotiating a contract with feelings attached. And that is not the kind of love anyone deserves to settle for.

4. When protecting your wealth is valid but not an excuse

Let's be real. If you've worked hard for your money, your assets, your career, or your business, you have every right to protect it. Nobody is saying you should just hand over the keys to your life the moment you fall in love. That would be irresponsible. Especially if you spent years building what you have before your partner ever showed up. Wanting security around your wealth does not make you heartless. It makes you wise.

But the part people don't talk about enough is this: protecting what you have cannot become a mask for avoiding partnership. It cannot be the reason you shut someone out of every decision, every account, every plan for the future. You don't get to claim love and still live like the other person is a stranger when it comes to your life's work. That's not love. That's just using protection as an excuse to keep all the power in your own hands.

There is a difference between being cautious and being closed. One is about safety and the other about control. One says, I want to be smart about how we build this. The other says, This is mine and you'll never be part of it. And the difference matters.

If you are entering a relationship with significant wealth, yes, get a prenup. Yes, be clear. Yes, protect what you created. But also take a good look at how your partner is contributing. Maybe not with money, but with time, care, emotional support, or stepping away from their own career to support yours. That counts. That matters. And that deserves to be seen on paper too.

A fair prenup protects both people. It does not punish someone for not being rich when they walked in. It does not act like the only thing worth protecting is what has a dollar sign next to it. If you are asking for protection, ask for it in a way that still honors the person you are building with. You don't need to give everything away. But if you are asking someone to share their life with you, to show up for you, to grow something with you, then your protection cannot look like a wall that shuts them out. That's not partnership. That's just fear with legal backing. Protect your wealth. Absolutely. But make sure you are not using that protection to excuse yourself from being generous, open, or fair. Because the moment you do, what you're protecting is no longer just money. It's your ego. And that will never keep a relationship whole.

5. The fine line between emotional safety and emotional manipulation

Everyone wants to feel safe in love. It's one of the most natural things to desire. To be with someone who makes you feel seen, understood, cared for, and protected. But sometimes what feels like safety is actually something else. Sometimes it's just quiet control. And by the time you notice, you've already learned how to keep yourself small just to keep the peace.

Emotional manipulation doesn't always come with yelling or cruelty. In fact, it often shows up with charm. With softness. With just the right words that sounds like love but leave you unsure of yourself. It looks like someone convincing you not to ask too many questions. Not to worry about the money. Not to bring up that concern again because it makes them uncomfortable. It looks like you slowly losing your confidence and calling it harmony.

6. If it is just his name on everything is it still your life?

You live there. You help take care of it. You make sure the fridge stays full, the bills get paid on time, the house feels like a home. You are in the photos. You are in the family group chat. You are beside him at every event, every dinner, every major moment. But when you look at the paperwork, the titles, the accounts, the business, the will, it is all in his name. Not yours. Not shared. Not even mentioned.

So what does that mean?

It means that while you are living the life together, the foundation of that life does not legally include you. And that is not just a detail. That is not just a formality. That is a message. A silent one, but loud in its meaning. It says, I love having you here, but I'm not planning for you to stay forever. It says, I want your support, your time, your energy, but I don't want you to have any real stake in what I've built.

This is where things get uncomfortable for a lot of people. Because it is easy to get caught up in the love, in the partnership, in the shared routine. You feel close, committed, bonded. And maybe you think asking questions about ownership would ruin the peace. Maybe you were taught not to care about those things. Maybe you think it is not romantic to talk about who owns what. If you are giving your life to someone, your time, your loyalty, your presence, you deserve to see yourself in the plan. You deserve to know where your name fits. Not just on Christmas cards and anniversary gifts, but on the documents that define security, legacy, and protection.

This is not about gold digging or being entitled, but about recognizing that love should not mean living invisibly inside someone else's empire. If he wants to build with you, then your name should show up. Somewhere. In the right places. Where it counts. Because otherwise, you are not in partnership. You are just visiting his life while being expected to act like it's yours too.

That is not fair. That is not safe. And it is not sustainable.

Love should never require you to disappear in order to feel included. And if everything you touch belongs to someone else, if every piece of the life you are helping maintain is signed under his name only, then eventually you have to ask yourself a hard question. Is this really my life? Or is it just the one I'm being allowed to borrow?

7. Why the law will not save you if the relationship was never fair to begin with

It will be unsafe to think that marriage will come with an automatic safety net, where the law becomes some sort of guardian in the background, and would step in the event of a divorce. If you build your life on this assumption, you'll find out how paper thin that safety net really is, when the dust settles. Marriage feels like something that comes with built-in rights, so it's easy to assume that the years you've invested, the sacrifices you've made, and the support you've offered will all naturally count when it's time to divide what you built together. It feels reasonable to expect that the big picture of your life will be recognized.

But the way relationships are handled legally relies a lot on clarity, documentation, and how you structured things while you were still together. The legal side of a partnership focuses on what can be shown and explained, especially when it comes to money, ownership, and shared responsibilities. It simply works with the information available, and that means your level of protection depends heavily on how your financial and personal decisions were arranged long before anything went wrong.

When a judge is asked to divide property or determine what belongs to each person, they have to follow a framework. They separate what was built during the marriage from what each person owned individually. They look at titles, accounts, financial records, and any agreements the couple made along the way. If your name was never added to a home, if you were never included in major financial decisions, or if there is no clear way to show how you contributed to the family's financial life, it becomes harder to reflect your role through the legal process. This isn't because your work wasn't real, but because the structure of the relationship didn't give it a place to stand.

Things also depend on where you live. In some states, anything earned or acquired during the marriage is automatically shared, no matter whose name is on it. Those places tend to lean toward a straightforward fifty-fifty split. In most other states, things are divided based on what seems fair for both people. Fairness doesn't always look like an even split. Judges are allowed to consider things like raising children, supporting a partner's career, how long the marriage lasted, each person's earning potential, and what the future may look like for both sides. The outcome can be thoughtful, but it still has to be connected to the reality the couple created on paper.

Support payments exist for situations where one partner stepped back from earning to keep the home running or to support the other person's progress. Courts look at the lifestyle the couple maintained, the length of the marriage, and the opportunities one person may have put on hold. But even here, the partner seeking support still needs to show how those choices created an imbalance. It isn't automatic simply because the marriage existed.

All of this is why the structure inside a relationship matters before any problems arise. If your name never appears on deeds or accounts, if you've never discussed ownership clearly, or if one person has held all the financial power for years, that imbalance often carries over when the relationship ends. Marriage on its own is not enough to protect someone who was never included in the practical decisions that shaped the couple's life.

You deserve recognition while the relationship is healthy. That means talking openly about shared ownership, making sure both names appear on documents where they should, and using tools that help create clarity. These conversations don't make a relationship transactional. They make it safer. They prevent misunderstandings later, and they help ensure that both partners are seen in the structure of the life they're building.

It also helps to keep track of anything that belongs to you individually so it doesn't get blended into the marriage in a way that complicates everything later. Records and clarity protect both partners, not just one. They make it easier for the legal side of things to reflect what you both already know to be true.

The legal process doesn't rewrite the story of the relationship. It reflects whatever framework the two of you created. When your daily life and your paperwork match, you're protected. When they don't line up, it becomes harder for anyone to fill in the gaps after the fact.

8. The truth about exit plans protecting without preparing for failure

Some people hear the words prenup or exit plan and immediately think the worst. They think you're expecting the relationship to fall apart. That the moment you start preparing for a "what if," you've already invited failure into the room.

Let's talk about what an exit plan actually is. It's not a breakup strategy, prediction or hidden message that you don't believe in the relationship. It's just preparation. The same way you buy insurance and hope you never need it. The same way you set aside emergency money, because life happens.

Having a clear plan for what happens if things don't work out is not a sign that you're planning to leave. It's a sign that you're showing up responsibly. It means you respect the relationship enough to make sure that even in the worst case scenario, both people can walk away with dignity. If that conversation makes your partner uncomfortable, it's worth asking why. Because a relationship that's truly healthy can handle the hard conversations. You can talk about what happens if things shift. You can look at the truth, not just the dream, and then plan with love, not fear.

The idea that love should be blindly trusting is one of the most damaging messages people grow up believing. Trust is important, yes. But real trust doesn't mean you leave yourself exposed. It means you take care of both of you, in every season, including the ones that might hurt. If the only way to prove your love is to ignore your own protection, then it is not love. It is performance. And eventually, you will feel it. You'll feel the imbalance. The silence. The fear of speaking up because it might make you seem cold or distant. And that's not a relationship. That's pressure dressed up as peace.

An exit plan is not a betrayal. It is actually a commitment that says, 'I care enough about you to make sure that if this ever changes, we don't destroy each other on the way out.' It says, I love you now, and I want to protect that love, even if one day we're no longer together.

9. Postnups - If you're already married and just waking up to all of this

So maybe you're reading all of this and thinking, well, that would have been great to know two years ago. Or five. Or twenty. Because you're already married. And there's no prenup. No structure. Just you, trying to figure out what's fair, and wondering if it's too late to protect yourself now.

It's not too late. It's just going to take a different kind of conversation.

That's where a *postnup* comes in. A postnuptial agreement is, in the simplest terms, a prenup signed after the wedding. But emotionally, it's not quite that simple. Because now you're not just planning for a future, you're already living in it. There's shared history. Shared finances. Maybe kids. Maybe a house. Maybe a whole pattern of one person being in control and the other one trying not to make things worse. Bringing up a postnup takes courage. It might sound like, I know we've already built a life, but I need to feel safe inside it. It might sound like, I love you, but I need to know that if anything ever happens, I won't be erased. And it's okay if those words feel heavy. They are heavy. But they're honest.

The moment you mention a postnup, some people think trouble is brewing, when in reality it doesn't signal anything of the sort. It actually means you care enough to fix what's been unspoken. It means you're not pretending anymore. It means you're ready to step into your marriage as a whole person, not just a supportive character in someone else's movie.

Legally, postnups can do many of the same things prenups do. They can define what's marital property and what's not. They can outline how finances will be handled if the relationship ends. They can create structure around businesses, investments, debt, or inheritance. And they can do it all while you're still very much together, still in love, still building. The key is the same as always: fairness. A postnup that's created under pressure, or presented like a demand, is likely to be challenged later. But if both people come to the table with open eyes and real care, it can be a way to reset. To realign. To say, maybe we didn't do this right the first time, but we're willing to do it better now.

And yes, sometimes the partner with more financial control resists the conversation. They say, Why now? What changed? Don't you trust me? And in that moment, you have to be strong enough to say, I've always trusted you. But now I also want to trust the structure we're living in. I want to trust that this love includes me, not just emotionally, but legally. Practically. Fully.

A postnup won't fix a broken relationship. But it can strengthen one that's ready to be honest. It can create a space where both people feel seen, protected, and responsible. And sometimes, that's all it takes to breathe new life into a marriage that was quietly starting to feel uneven.

So no, it's not too late. You can ask. You can talk. You can draft something fair. You can step into your own life more clearly, even if the wedding was years ago. Start the conversation, because you finally understand what it means to stay completely, safely, and on equal ground.

10. Closing the gap: How to create love and legal structure that coexist without crushing each other

A lot of people think love and legal structure don't go together. Like once you bring in a lawyer or a contract, the romance dies. Like talking about property or bank accounts means you've stopped thinking with your heart and started thinking like a cold business-person. And that right there is the problem. We've been taught to believe that real love is all emotion and no logic, and that the moment we ask for clarity, we've somehow poisoned the relationship. But that's not true. Love without structure is like building a house with no foundation. Sure, it might look pretty for a while. You might decorate it, host people in it, grow in it. But the moment a storm comes, everything shakes. And if there's no base holding it all together, it falls. Slowly, at first. Then all at once.

What we need to start saying out loud is that it's not wrong to want both. It's not wrong to want to feel deeply and think clearly. It's not wrong to be madly in love and still want your name on the deed. You're not less loyal for asking questions. You're not less romantic for wanting to know how things work behind the scenes. You're not difficult, or cold, or greedy for saying, I want to be protected too.

There is a big difference between creating security and controlling someone. Between protecting your legacy and hiding your money. Between planning your future and making sure the other person never has a voice in it. If your love can't hold the weight of a hard conversation, then it's not as strong as it looks on the outside.

So how do you close the gap? Stop pretending that love will figure everything out on its own. You sit down. You talk. Not just when you're upset or scared, but when things are going well. That's the best time, actually. When you're both happy, grounded, clear-minded. You ask, what do we want to build? What are we bringing to the table? What do we both need to feel safe?

You make space for the other person to speak honestly, even if it's uncomfortable. You don't take it personally if they say they want their own bank account or need a backup plan. You don't weaponize their fear as a reason to question their loyalty. You look at them, not through the lens of control, but with the eyes of someone who truly wants them to stay - freely, safely, completely.

Love and legal structure are not enemies. They're just two sides of the same commitment. One side says, I feel this. The other says, I'll protect it. And when you have both, you stop walking on eggshells. You stop hoping things never change just to avoid chaos. You start building something you can both stand on, for real.

When you create a relationship where legal clarity and emotional safety coexist, something amazing happens. You trust each other more. You stop guessing. You stop trying to read between the lines. You rest, because everything is in the open. That is what love deserves.

Afterword

Reaching the end of this book brings one truth into full light: relationships do not thrive on emotion alone. They survive, grow, and stay balanced because both people choose clarity over assumption, structure over guesswork, and honesty over silence. Love may set the direction, but it is the decisions you make that shape the security of your future.

The heart of everything you've learned comes down to this simple reality. A relationship is both an emotional bond and a shared life with real responsibilities. When couples ignore the practical side of that life, they might be avoiding discomfort, but inviting uncertainty. And uncertainty is what turns small cracks into deep fractures. The smartest thing any couple can do is make sure their emotional world and their practical world match. When those two align, the relationship becomes stronger, not strained; and safer, not fragile.

Fairness is not something you beg for at the end. It is something you build consistently, quietly, and intentionally while everything is still good. It is created in the choices you make together, the conversations you refuse to postpone, and the clarity you agree to put in writing. Nothing about this is unromantic. It is the highest form of care because it protects both partners from confusion, resentment, and imbalance. It keeps the relationship grounded, even when life shifts in ways no one expects.

Clarity does not predict separation. It prevents regret, preserves trust, and reminds you that your commitment deserves more than hope, it deserves structure. When you understand this, you'll stop seeing these conversations as threats and start seeing them as tools that honor your partnership.

If there is anything to take with you from these pages, let it be the confidence to build your relationship with intention. Let it be the courage to protect your future with the same tenderness you use to protect your love. And let it be the understanding that security is not something that arrives at the end. It is something you create, piece by piece, while the relationship is still strong.

Love grows best inside a life that is clearly built. When you treat both the heart and the foundation with equal care, you give your relationship the chance to last without fear, without confusion, and without leaving either partner unprotected. That is the kind of future you deserve.

www.ingramcontent.com/pod-product-compliance
Lightning Source LLC
LaVergne TN
LVHW022323200926
848481LV00004B/1406